i-SPY

my own birds

quack!

SPY IT! STICK IT!

Published by **Collins** An imprint of HarperCollins Publishers
Westerhill Road, Bishopbriggs, Glasgow G64 2QT
www.harpercollins.co.uk

HarperCollins Publishers
Macken House, 39/40 Mayor Street Upper, Dublin 1,
D01 C9W8, Ireland

Publisher: Michelle I'Anson
Editorial lead: Gillian Bowman
Designer: Kevin Robbins
Layout: Jouve
Editorial: Janice McNeillie, Lauren Reid, Carol Medcalf

ISBN 9780008562656

Printed in India

10 9 8 7 6 5 4 3 2 1

Acknowledgements
All images used under license from Shutterstock.com.

How to use your i-SPY book

Look out for the things in the book.

If you spy it, put a sticker in the circle.

Keep your eyes peeled for Top Spots. These are hard to find, so you'll have to search high and low to see them.

Ask a grown up to help you add up your points. When you score 100 points, you get your super spotter sticker!

Blue tit

STICK IT!

1 point

Lapwing

TOP SPOT!

3 points

SUPER SPOTTER

Note to grown up

Send in for your FREE i-SPY progress poster, where your child can stick their super-spotter stickers!

Head to collins.co.uk/i-SPY for details

Parks and gardens

If you look out of a window wherever you are you may see one of these birds.

Robin

STICK IT!

1 point

Blackbird

STICK IT!

2 points

House sparrow

STICK IT!

1 point

Blackbirds have a very musical song. The female is dark brown.

Collared dove

STICK IT!
1 point

Greenfinch

TOP SPOT!
3 points

Common wood pigeon

STICK IT!
1 point

The woodpigeon is the largest type of pigeon in the UK.

Wren

STICK IT!
2 points

If you have a pair of binoculars these can help with birdwatching as you can see things that are far away.

Starling

STICK IT!

2 points

Blue tit

STICK IT!

1 point

Blue tits have blue heads and great tits have black heads.

Great tit

STICK IT!

1 point

Long-tailed tit

TOP SPOT!

3 points

This small bird has... a long tail!

Chaffinch

STICK IT!

2 points

Pied wagtail

STICK IT!

1 point

Song thrush

STICK IT!

2 points

On the farm

Some birds on the farm or in the countryside give us eggs and poultry but some find the perfect place to nest.

Barn owl

TOP SPOT!

3 points

Owls are very quiet when they fly.

Chicken

STICK IT!

1 point

There are more chickens in the world than people.

Turkey

STICK IT!

2 points

Pheasant

STICK IT!

1 point

When a peacock
spreads out its
wings the patterns
look like eyes.

Goose

STICK IT!

1 point

Peacock

STICK IT!

2 points

Fields and hedges

These birds love eating berries, seeds and grain found in fields and bushes.

Swift

STICK IT!

2 points

Swifts can fly as fast as a car on a motorway.

Goldfinch

STICK IT!

2 points

Goldfinches have sharp beaks so they can get seeds out of thistles.

Magpie

STICK IT!

1 point

Carrion crow

STICK IT!

1 point

Swallow

STICK IT!

2 points

Swallows visit the UK in the summer and fly to a warmer country for the winter.

Lapwing

TOP SPOT!

3 points

Hooded crow

STICK IT!

1 point

On the water

In rivers and lakes you can see these birds swimming or diving in the water.

If the weather is right these geese can fly 1,500 miles in a day!

Canada goose

STICK IT!

1 point

Mute swan

STICK IT!

1 point

Mallard duck

Male mallard ducks have a green head, the female ducks are brown.

STICK IT!

1 point

Moorhen

STICK IT!

2 points

Tufted duck

STICK IT!

2 points

Herons have very long legs!

Heron

STICK IT!

2 points

Kingfisher

TOP SPOT!

3 points

Kingfishers look like small electric-blue arrows when they fly.

On the shore

These birds all live by the sea where they can find their favourite things to eat.

Common gull

Look out for their bright orange legs!

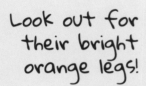

STICK IT!

1 point

Redshank

STICK IT!

2 points

Common sandpiper

STICK IT!

2 points

Dunlin

STICK IT!

1 point

Shag

STICK IT!

1 point

Terns fly long distances and dive to catch fish and insects.

Common tern * *
*

TOP SPOT!

3 points

Oystercatcher

STICK IT!

1 point

On the cliffs

Cliffs are a safe place for birds to raise their chicks.

Kittiwake

TOP SPOT!

3 points

They like to nest at the top of a cliff.

Puffin

TOP SPOT!

3 points

Cormorant

STICK IT!

1 point

Guillemot

STICK IT!

2 points

Guillemots look like penguins.

A gannet is the largest seabird.

Gannet

STICK IT!

2 points

Razorbill

STICK IT!

2 points

Birds of prey

Birds use their feathers to be able to fly, but they also act as camouflage which can make them harder to see.

These small birds can hover in the air while looking for prey!

Kestrel

STICK IT!

2 points

Sparrowhawk

STICK IT!

2 points

Osprey

TOP SPOT!

3 points

These graceful birds dive into lakes to catch fish.

Buzzard

STICK IT!

1 point

Golden eagle

TOP SPOT!

3 points

19

Songbirds

You usually hear birds before you see them! Each bird has a unique and beautiful song.

Goldcrest

TOP SPOT!

3 points

Goldcrests are the UK's smallest birds!

Nightingale

TOP SPOT!

3 points

Skylark

STICK IT!

2 points

Turtle dove

STICK IT!

1 point

Blackcap

STICK IT!
2 points

Dunnock

STICK IT!
1 point

Chiffchaff

STICK IT!
2 points

The chiffchaff's song sounds like its name.

In the woods

If you walk quietly through a wood you may hear some of these birds moving in the trees.

Treecreeper

Treecreepers walk up trees, eating insects in the bark.

STICK IT!

2 points

Jackdaw

STICK IT!

1 point

Jay

STICK IT!

2 points

Tawny owl

STICK IT!

2 points

Nuthatch

STICK IT!

2 points

Can you hear woodpeckers drilling the trees with their beaks?

Greater spotted woodpecker

TOP SPOT!

3 points

Bird care

If you feed the birds they will come and visit you to have their dinner. Don't forget to leave out some water!

People without gardens can still feed the birds using window feeders.

Fat ball

STICK IT!

1 point

Bird table

STICK IT!

2 points

Bird bath

STICK IT!

2 points

Birds use bird baths to drink water, have a bath and splash in the water!

Bird box

STICK IT!

2 points

Peanuts

STICK IT!

1 point

Dovecote

TOP SPOT!

3 points

Meal worms

STICK IT!

1 point

Doves and pigeons like to nest in dovecotes.

Bird words

If you see eggs in a nest you should never touch them.

Birds grow new feathers at least once a year.

Feather

A colony is where lots of birds live together.

Bird poo

STICK IT!
1 point

Wing

STICK IT!
1 point

Clutch * * *

TOP SPOT!
* * 3 points

Egg

STICK IT!
2 points

Beak

Birds do not have any teeth.

STICK IT!
1 point

A clutch is the name for lots of eggs laid together in one nest.

Baby birds

Baby birds need a lot of food and sleep to grow. Can you guess what birds these babies will grow up to be?

Chick

STICK IT!

1 point

Owlet

** *

TOP SPOT!

* *

3 points

Duckling

STICK IT!

1 point

Gosling

STICK IT!

2 points

When goslings hatch from their egg, they will follow the first thing they see.

Cygnet

STICK IT!

2 points

Nestling

STICK IT!

2 points

Fledgling

STICK IT!

2 points

A nestling is a young bird still in the nest, a fledgling is old enough to leave its nest.

At the zoo

In a zoo you can see birds that live in other parts of the world. Some will be in a large cage called an aviary.

Little egret

STICK IT!

1 point

Mandarin duck

STICK IT!

2 points

Flamingos eat with their heads upside down!

Rhinoceros hornbill

STICK IT!

2 points

Flamingo

STICK IT!

1 point

arrot

STICK IT!

1 point

Ostrich

STICK IT!

2 points

Ostriches are the world's largest birds.

Penguin

STICK IT!

1 point

A snowy owl's feet is covered with feathers, like fluffy slippers.

Snowy owl

TOP SPOT!

3 points

What else can you spot?

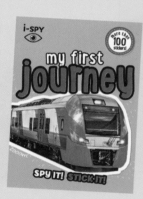

Get little ones started on their very own spotting adventure with My First i-SPY sticker books! Packed with fun facts and photographs to keep children entertained. To see the full collection, go to collins.co.uk/i-spy